The *Panda* Syndrome

A Societal Imposition

Frank Simonelli

BALBOA
PRESS
A DIVISION OF HAY HOUSE

ISBN: 978-1-4525-6346-6 (sc)
ISBN: 978-1-4525-6347-3 (e)

Library of Congress Control Number: 2012921838

Balboa Press books may be ordered through booksellers or by contacting:

Balboa Press
A Division of Hay House
1663 Liberty Drive
Bloomington, IN 47403
www.balboapress.com
1-(877) 407-4847

Because of the dynamic nature of the Internet, any web addresses or links contained in this book may have changed since publication and may no longer be valid. The views expressed in this work are solely those of the author and do not necessarily reflect the views of the publisher, and the publisher hereby disclaims any responsibility for them.

The author of this book does not dispense medical advice or prescribe the use of any technique as a form of treatment for physical, emotional, or medical problems without the advice of a physician, either directly or indirectly. The intent of the author is only to offer information of a general nature to help you in your quest for emotional and spiritual well-being. In the event you use any of the information in this book for yourself, which is your constitutional right, the author and the publisher assume no responsibility for your actions.

Any people depicted in stock imagery provided by Thinkstock are models, and such images are being used for illustrative purposes only.
Certain stock imagery © Thinkstock.

Printed in the United States of America

Balboa Press rev. date: 1/24/2013

Contents

Foreword

Life presents us with many challenges. For some, these may be physical, others mental, emotional, financial or spiritual, nonetheless, all daily struggles that must be addressed. For most, it has become easier to turn a blinds eye to these challenges rather than face them head on resulting in a loss of our individuality due to accepting what we fear we cannot change.

Conformity has become the reason we, as spiritual beings, are losing sight of what is important, what is vital, to a healthy loving relationship with not only ourselves but those we love and interact with throughout our lifetime. As a loving wife and dedicated mother, I have found that this life affords us wondrous experiences as well as much pain and sorrow and when society speaks, all too often, we listen.

In Frank Simonelli's *The Panda Syndrome, A Societal Imposition,* he reintroduces us to who we truly are by expressing what most only think to themselves. This collection has not only altered the way he looks at himself and life but it is an inspiration for anyone who reads it. This collection is for anyone who has lost their self-worth, their dignity or has just been caught up in this experience we call life. His analytical and unique perspective on society and its impact upon the human spirit evokes many questions concerning society, humanity, God, faith and love. He has taken an introspective look within himself and through his findings, I, as have many others, been shown how to regain control over their right to happiness.

Being gifted as a clairvoyant from birth, he struggled with acceptance, always feeling "Different." Today, he accepts this gift but chooses to use this ability in a personal way rather than publicly. This gift, along with his truly loving soul and uncanny way with words has taught me how to seek out the truths within my own floundering soul and broken heart. He leads a path back to the reality of what we should be and must be in order to thrive as spiritual beings on this beautiful planet that at times, can prove to be not so beautiful.

He is such an inspiration to both me and to those that have known him. He has given us the hope of better tomorrows. The ability to understand and learn from our experiences and then the ability to sever the past enabling us to propel forward, freeing the anchors that hold us down, as well as the gift of being truly grateful for each new day that is bestowed upon us. I wait with much anticipation to see what the next leg of his life's journey will inspire him to pen.

With much admiration and love,

Doreen

Preface

"The streaming white light descends upon thee as the winds of divine wisdom fill thy wings. Permit thee thine freedom. Allow it to carry thee home. Encircle thee as I ascend into your loving arms, for I am consumed in the warmth of your embrace. Nothing of you shall I ever ask again, for I am weightless. Alas, thine freedom is at hand."

All I ever wanted was a better understanding of why I was here in this unusual place. How I got here and when I would be leaving. Almost immediately my curiosities were compressed by my ideological parents, the hypocritical Catholics who were more interested in their social acceptance than they were in my individuality. As a result of my curiosity, I quickly became a burden to them. I had many questions and as I grew, I set out to answer as many of the questions as I could. Who exactly is God? Have you ever met Him? How do you know He is a him and not a her? All this and I was only five years old sitting in a pew asking an annoyed parishioner who eventually moved. I place the donation in the basket anyway as my mother told me to. Nonetheless, I searched on. I discovered that many religions existed and different ethnicities as well. There were so many steadfast opinions of this god who actually scared the shit out of everyone and yet with all this confusion, I always felt this divinity within myself, this internal love, a voice that spoke to me, a truly loving spirit that I would learn to rely on during the course of my life.

Through the years I discovered truths in our human behavior. I learned to conform in order to survive. I earned a substantial income; purchased the things I wanted and created an image for you to accept. However, I lost myself and my freedoms in doing so. I suppressed my love of art, music and literature. I denounced my gift of clairvoyance so not to be exposed by those I intended to impress. Several times in my life I have met people who saw through the mask and tried to pry the free spirit out from within a societal imprisonment but I hid my insecurities and fell back into the shadows. Fate would have none of it, so again my thoughts were to question and discover. I was inspired to release that which I held inside for so long but the journey has taken its toll. I am grateful for such gifts. As a result of my relationships, I have become motivated to express my experiences with you.

It is not my intention to mock God or any religious faith, only to express the way I have come to feel about my life's journey as well as the way others have expressed to me the way that they secretly feel about life, love, religion and the American culture. We all have been affected and through my research I have found that we're really not all that different.

I hope these short stories and poems remind you of who you really are. I hope you question everything; after all, it is your birth right to exist and to discover your individual meaningful purpose. No two lives shall ever be the same nor were they ever meant to be.

FCS

Acknowledgments

To Mr. Oberman, I will always be grateful to my art teacher. His dedication, friendship and belief in my work will always be cherished. I hope you're not disappointed.

To my wife, Doreen, there are no words that can describe my gratitude or my eternal love.

To one who shall remain anonymous, I am forever grateful to you for unlocking the cage.

An Existence

My contentment is obviously inconsequential.
My spiritual existence provides no meaningful contribution.
My human presence is nothing more than a face amid an angry mob.
My charitable donation never seems to reach those in need, nor can I
ever donate enough to please their gods.
My questions incite anger within the clergy,
my thoughts appear to challenge in defiance.
I am unacceptable to the unapproachable,
those who speak the Word in a human voice.
Nor shall I ever be embraced by the
ideological worshipers who I have previously supported but now
distance themselves from the essence of my human presence.
If I were to tally my total existence,
there would appear to be less and less of me each day.
My time here is very short apparently.
Society spends me frivolously.

So where lay the truths?
What is the point of my momentary existence
and to whom should it matter that I exist at all?
Surely the world could do without another philosophical prophet.
However, I do not peddle any false promises
of something greater beyond the greater good.
I merely seek answers to the many questions that have risen
from my life's experiences.
However, my thoughts it seems, bear no plausible meanings.
I am told that they are nothing more than contrary denouncements
of the proven truth.
My questions are imprisoned by ridicule.
My words, absolute blasphemy!

Perhaps, I have meaning to those who lurk conspicuously
in my fading shadow, waiting to feed off the fruits of my labor.
The inept; themselves, those who do not bear the courage,
less the capability, to ever exert a greater force against that which
censors their free will.
Perhaps, I do not have anything to say on their behalf,
for I have been abandoned by them long ago.
My words, it seems, continue to fall upon deaf ears;
And they cannot be refuted, for their tongues have been severed.
However, I know you and I know that you can hear me.

Of the cold and timid souls who have surrendered their birth right
to exist without free will,
they are sequestered by the very idols who rule them.
Those who never seem to be impressed by your presence,
traveling along the path that has been carved out,
the predetermined course for a predictable life,
accepting and regurgitating whatever they are served.
The bitter feast laid out upon the table of conformity.

No map is required, for only one exit exists.
No menu shall be provided, for the morsels have been rationed.
The whole ambiguous journey has been compromised by the
conformists who preceded them,
the martyrs who sacrificed the lambs.
Theirs is merely a point to point existence as the ancestral
line slowly moves closer to the edge of the eternal abyss
and only seeks the approval of their peers.
Nor shall they ever experience the contentment of freedom and
individuality within a conscious mortality.

Angel Astray - Spirit in Exile

The sun scantily staggered into the contemptible sky.
The stars surrendered their swords and turned away
as the angels remorsefully wept and bowed their heads in shame.

With painful humiliation, the November moon summoned the
courage to show its face, as the final light succumbed to the eternal darkness.
The human conflict raged on and on, day upon day, night upon night.
Mortally wounded by societal persecution, the rebellious burden
quietly subsides and is finally set free.

His tormented spirit immediately vacates its earthly imprisonment
and ascends high above the distant horizon where the sun meets the sky.
He leaves behind only decaying, lifeless remains and its fleeting
memories of this unfathomable life.
Then the essence of his being shall rejoin the living earth only to be reborn once
again...

"To know me is to love me," he once said. A grim reminder of the
loneliness that he brought upon himself.
After all, who ever truly knew him?
A disturbing thought! Nonetheless, I admired him.
I attempted to uncover the many layers of his life and reach the
complex thoughts that were reserved and stored protectively deep
within him.
I searched tirelessly for the truths and meanings of such profound
wisdom.

A written collection of observations and assessments of us and this
place

during his time here remain. A testament to his extraordinary existence.

I can still recall the ominous stillness and the haunting quiet of his vast, echoing, brick and steel tomb, perched high above the city dwellers. The howling, icy cold winds and the unrelenting heavy rain continued rapping on the old, iron- framed, stained glass windows like a mob of angry protesters, demanding retribution for their loss.

As I walked around, the worn- down floor boards creaked eerily, stopping me nervously in my tracks. I continued, reluctantly, to have a look around.
It appeared that all of his belongings lay wherever he last left them, everything in scattered disarray.
I stumbled upon his unfinished works of art and literature.
There, penned on so many crumpled and wrinkled pages were his thoughts of this life. So many stories, so many incomplete and, apparently, all untold.

I find it so troubling to think that no one shall ever come to know this man, nor shall they ever have been able to comprehend the complexity of his thoughts and philosophies, yet I find myself privileged to hear the message in every word he said. I recall, some time ago, he said to me:

"The human experience is not one single defined purpose for all, contrary, for each one of us it has its own individual purpose, your own life, your birth right to exist and to experience this wondrous place.
Each life, unique and special, each one, contributing to another's experience, be it good or bad." He went on to say,

"For one to take, another must be willing to give.
For one to flourish, another must perish.
For one to feel love, another must take up arms in rage.
Each independently serving himself and his fateful purpose, simultaneously contributing to the human experience.
What will set you apart from them is discovering the truth in who you are

and embracing it.

We are all aware of the mysterious spirit within ourselves and it challenges us to come to know it and accept it.

This is your soul speaking to your spirit offering its guidance and experience.

Of all things in this life, the subject of love is the most difficult to begin to assess or ever comprehend; it is the driving force of the entire universe."

He continued,

"Love is the greatest of all power. It is found at the center of all things, good and bad.

You must discover the love within yourself and use it for a better good.

To understand love, would be to say you understand God and that is totally illogical. No one shall ever comprehend God or love."

How foolish of us to ever dare to say we understand the subject matter.

However, he did say,

"For one to honor the loving spirit of God one must learn to honor himself and then be willing to give of oneself without need of recognition or compensation." This, he said, is the birthplace of unconditional love.

Our conversations were unlike anything else that I had ever come to know, so profound, so compelling. Perhaps that is why he kept to himself.

He was unwilling to offer his love and he was unwilling to give of himself for fear of misinterpretation.

However, he did share these thoughts with me for many years.

His words were a gift, and they were spoken with love and passion, perhaps, he had me fooled.

Such naivety, in retrospect, he must have discovered his purpose.

He said,

"There can be no toils where there are no conflicts,
where there are no debates, where there is no interaction."
Yet, here in this place of total solitude, the quiet place where he dwelled,
the conflicts and debates raged on it seems.
It never appeared to me that any truths were ever discovered,
nor was there any acceptance ever exhibited.
The only truth uncovered here was that a wonderful man, his pathetic,
tormented spirit, never actually belonged here in the first place.

Perhaps, an angel that fell down out of heaven.
Whatever he was, he was not of this world.
I will always be grateful to have been able to interact with him in my life.
His lessons were extraordinary!
I hope his spirit continues to guide me to where it is he is from.

I have committed myself to writing about all that I have shared with
and learned from this incomparable soul.
In his words and thoughts, I found a commonality that I think we all
share.

I hope that at some point you will come to appreciate his poetry, his
philosophy and his wisdom as I have.

After all, every one of us has a unique individual purpose and perhaps,
through him, I have discovered mine.
Who knows, maybe someday we will speak again.

The Height of Arrogance
The Fall from Freedom

I climb atop the coping that covers the parapet,
I'm standing 1,368 feet above my troubles,
looking out over that which I shall never possess.
The air above the shattered city fills my senses.
The sun shall fall from the heavens for a final time.
The soft blue sky; aflame behind the towers of tinsel and glaze,
below me I can hear the screams and prayers, the
voices in anguish of a life that must continue on without me.
It is only now that I realize how insignificant my existence is.
No one knows that I'm here.
The heat and the thick toxic air, overpowering.
The acceptance of my mortality is clear.
Should I hold my breath, or should I scream out loud?
My conscious challenges my judgment.
However, the only choice becomes painfully obvious.
In a final coherent moment, I ask myself, "Have I gone mad?"
Perhaps not, for I exercise my right of liberty,
for freedom, it seems, comes with a great price.
After all, in America, no one is truly free.

Into Darkness

A cold chill runs down his contorted spine,
freezing the infected viciousness he holds inside.
Involuntarily, a sigh of disgust is expelled in subconscious objection
as he unwillingly breathes in another breath,
signaling the commencement of the next pointless day.
Darkness bleeds through the panes of obscured glass
where the bright rays of sunlight once streamed in to warm
the enthusiastic spirit sheltered within the soul.
The coarse, unshaven, placid face and uncombed hair in scattered
disarray is a stark reminder of what his life has become.
Not a trace of evidence remains of this extraordinary being,
not even his inaccessible, unrealistic goals.
Even the loneliness sheds not a tear as the tormented silent reflection
angrily peers back at him.
Devoid of any human emotion,
a determined unwillingness to exist any further,
he is tortured by this unrelenting mortal experience.
The sadness fills the void with the deepest emptiness.
He quietly returns to sit once again,
in the old worn creaking wooden chair,
staring out upon the bleak dismal early morning rain
as it falls softly onto the trees shadowed by a dark villainous
sky from whence it came.
A smoldering cigarette clenched tightly between his decaying teeth
glows eerily in the ominous darkness of his tomb.
The stench of vile smoke fills the room,
and is eventually absorbed by the silence.
The ghostly haunting memories of his youth beckon him to return
to that which promised a prosperous future, no longer threatens him.
His mind is no longer consumed with anger and rage.
Even the most precious of memories are distorted,

twisted into the lies that have become the misfortunes upon
his journey.

He cannot grieve the life he lost to his own fears and insecurities.

The internal, horrific struggle no longer ensues.

However, it does not require courage to challenge one's own truths,
only to face and accept the truths for what they are.

He slowly slips beneath the cover of self- righteous pity.

He breathed his last mortal breath as the vapors of his existence
fade into the darkness that haunted him.

The Sea of Despair

I am beginning to find it difficult to distinguish
the difference between my own reality and that
part of my imagination that was just a fantasy.
I speak not of the realization of my dreams,
for the rain of tears has dissolved all of what could have been,
flooding them like a torrent river into
the deep dark sea of sorrow.
I no longer possess the strength to continue
treading in the thick murky ocean of my sadness.
There is no tide, no waves,
that shall reach the shore, no beacon of hope to guide me,
only the solemn stillness of my own despair.
Although hearts and hands reach out,
I find neither the strength, nor the notion
that there is actually something left of me to be saved.
Selfish gestures perhaps,
if only to enable them to justify themselves,
but then it is the human compassion that solicits such heroic acts.
The once beautiful satin blue sky that stared down
upon me during my passionate youth is now
the cold, dark, overcast veil of truth that which
causes the painful involuntary trembling.
Freezing the spirit within, mortally extinguishing its light.
The once productive and creative mind,
now, idle and blank with no need of any further contribution.
What remains now, is the severely contorted memory
of the fantasy that was once myself.
With eyes wide open, sight fading to black,
silently slipping beneath the sea of despair.

Cause and Effect

How has my life become like this?
Did I take on too much?
Was there something I missed?
I look back at what I could have been.
I live with what I've become and all of my sins.
They say it's all prewritten, that it's all preset.
They say it's all cause and effect.
There is no coincidence; it's all etched in stone
and when She's ready,
she will send in the Angels to fly me back home.
So I continue on with this journey the best way that I can.
I bear little contentment; after all, I am all that I am.
So don't tell me it's all just cause and effect.
Because my life has become a disaster and I'm fucking upset!
There is no coincidence; it's all etched in stone
and before too long, I'll be heading back Home.
Yes, I'll have many questions when it comes time for me.
The list will be long; but it won't really matter
because best of all, I'll be free.
So for now, I'll be here roaming around.

I'll cause and effect while I'm still above ground.

Who's to Blame

Sadly, I regret to report that this life,
once filled with enthusiastic optimism
and euphoric dreams of all that could
be accomplished in such a wondrous place,
has amounted to nothing more than a
broken heart and shattered dreams.

Such delusional thoughts,
I have to admit, considering my current
state of affairs, had I known that my
dreams were so fragile, I would have
taken better care to protect them from
the evil forces and the corrosive elements
that set out to destroy such fantasies.

As for the broken heart, perhaps, I would
have been of better judgment to not have
allowed anyone besides myself to have
and to hold such a precious commodity.
I can see now that I was completely
unprepared to meet the challenges of
the inconceivable reality that is this world.

What makes me the most sad is that I
allowed all these things, the whole infected,
mindless process to occur in my life.
I shall never expect of myself, to attempt
to place the burden of blame upon those
who deliberately contributed to my existence
in a negative fashion.

Nor shall I in the same way ever surrender any
accolades or credits to those who truly believe
that they, in all their goodness, helped me
achieve my unrealistic goals during the
course of my life.

Regardless of who is to blame, I admit that
I created all of this alone.
After all, I took the chances,
I made the choices, some fickle
and some very calculated.
Nonetheless, all of my own free will.
The results, I must say, are abundantly obvious.
Sadly, I regret to report that my life is nothing more
than it is, because of me!

Shadow of Mortal Love

Thread of finality thou dost sever.
Angelic breath falls silent,
words unspoken now and forever.
Eternity awaits thy spirit.
Alas, the warmth of divine light draws thee in.
Earthly bonds thou hast broken.
Silhouette frightened by shadow,
cast upon the road thou hast chosen.
The wilted, crimson velvet petals fall softly
to the floor, free from threat of thorn.
So gently lifted by breath of sigh,
harmless and untethered.
To thee, once a symbol of love thou hast gifted.
So go, slip beneath the veil of mortal darkness,
into deepest slumber.
For thou shan't wait for thee.
Go now, dance among the young stars of flickering light,
high above in the vast heavens,
in the deepest darkness of night.
Never stray so far, or beyond my sight.
Thy love survives throughout eternity.
The endless beam of light thou shall speed,
not of life, not of dreams, two souls divide.
No pain of mortal loss shall I grieve.

Vulnerable Wisdom

The complexity of thought can lead to the premature demise of one's mind. Wisdom, however, comes at great cost. I have discovered that the deeper I explore my emotions, the more emotional I become, thus negating any wisdom I have accrued and coherently put to use. For the complexity of emotion comes from a place far outside the realm of thinking where even the wisest of men fail the test. Where the strongest of men, are easily defeated and where the simplest of men cower and surrender in shame. All of whom are afflicted by the insecurity of vulnerability. Hence, the complexity of emotion can ultimately cause the total demise of one's existence as it relates to pain and suffering. There can be no wisdom detected where there are thoughts of bringing end to such pain and there is no logic where these very emotions overwhelm such wisdom.

Is it logical to assume that there is a point in achieving any comprehension of the human emotion love? Wise men travel great distances across the seas of knowledge and never arrive upon the shores of wisdom. They spend themselves selfishly in the pursuit of this deep knowledge which we often misinterpret as the greatest of wisdoms.

Wisdom is like a flawless diamond, the raw material exists, if one searches long enough, he may stumble across it. Ironically, he may never know that he holds this diamond in his hands. Exposing the flawless gem is the same as saying I have acquired much knowledge, never cutting away the useless material and exposing the perfection within.

Wisdom is the perfection of knowledge through thought, truths, logic and the deepest understanding of facts we can prove beyond doubt, thought produced from cold hard datum and completely uninfluenced by any human emotion. So then, is that to say that a person who exudes extraordinary erudition, he of immeasurable wisdom, is incapable of love? After all, where there is true wisdom, there cannot exist, any fantasies, only problems and solutions, calculations and equations. Would it be logical to assume that I am completely incapable of love? Does one who loves lack the mental capability of achieving great wisdom, or is none the wiser?

How can there be any logic in love without vulnerable wisdom? Yet some of life's great lessons do not necessarily come from a book or a university. Some things are discovered within oneself. To truly begin to comprehend the emotions associated with love one must somehow learn to coexist with his heart and mind and try to comprehend his own loving emotions without fear of vulnerability. Perhaps one who has accrued great wisdom is never truly wise. For no one is wiser than one who loves unconditionally. I yearn for a better understanding of this notion. I find myself exhausted by the complexity of these agonizing thoughts.

For the Last Time

Part 1

You fucked me over for the last time!
My God, is this the end; is this really the end of it all?
How the fuck do you justify yourself?
What the fuck are you?
Cold, heartless, miserable, is this the real you?
Do you take pride in the pain you cause?
Do you create and destroy?
Love then hate?
Do you enjoy watching a soul perish?
How fucking twisted can you be!
What's the point of you at all?
Who wants to be part of anything else there might be after this
bullshit?
The joke has to have a punch line for it to end,
but no, this joke continues on and on, again and again.
Raise one up then crash him down,
make him crawl, this is how you teach?
This is your love?
Why come to me at all?
Go on and fuck over someone else, what more do you want?
What game do you play?
This is the end, it has to be!
I ask for nothing, you give nothing.
I raise up a crop and you send locust.
I plant a seed, you provide no rain.
When I hurt inside you're the pain!
Take it all away, what does it matter?
It's all in your hands after all, so do what you will.
My faith is shattered!

One's Will

Part 2

On a dark rainy evening, I was on my way home when the subtle
sound of thunder began to rumble and I realized I was alone.
I noticed the shadow of a man as he passed me by.
I knew there was a storm forming above me in the night sky.
As the lightning crackled it made a horrific hiss,
the rain fell heavily and it created an eerie mist.
So I ducked into a doorway behind an old brownstones stair,
my clothing was saturated and so was my hair.

There was something about Him that seemed familiar to me.
I don't know what it was exactly but I had to try and see.
That's when I realized I'd been here before because
I remembered the old tavern, the cobblestone street,
and a stack of old newspapers that laid by a door.
I tried so hard to get a better look at His face,
but something frightened me,
there was something eerily familiar about this place.

The faceless man just walked on by,
as the torrential rain fell from a thunderous sky.
He seemed completely unfazed as the rain pelted Him.
I noticed His clothing wasn't wet nor was His skin.
Just then He stopped along-side an old street light.
He turned slowly towards me and I thought that He might.
I tried to stare Him down as He moved to approach.
God, there was something about Him that looked like a ghost!
Oh man, this is crazy, as I thought to myself!
Should I just stand here and panic or should I yell out for help?
He stopped in front of me and He looked around.

He then waved me over and pointed to the ground.
With a deep hollow voice, I remember He said...

"Come and walk with me and we'll talk about all the
thoughts you have in your head."

He already knew me so there's no point to hide.
Deep in my soul, I felt him inside.
I continued on talking while I kept up the pace.
I looked right at Him and yet, I never saw His face.
I asked Him to explain to me what my life was about.
Then I took a deep breath because I knew with no doubt,
this was the moment, I'd know tonight,
if it all ends here or if I'd continue the fight.
The thunder stopped rumbling, the sky no longer flashed.
Somehow I knew He'd start with my past.

"This is the life you chose," He went on to say.
"It was up to you to live it and you made it this way.
You chose a line and blazed a path,
it all added up and you did the math.
Now you've arrived at this time and place.
The best you can do is curse My existence and surrender your faith.
I have a good mind to take you back and you know I could,
but before I do you will understand me and all that is good.
From here on in you'll do My will.
There will be many questions
but I promise this prophecy will be fulfilled.
Now make your choice, I don't have much time to explain
and you only have ten minutes to catch your train.
It will take you back to the life that you know,
the one you regret and have nothing to show.
However, if you take My hand and walk along-side of me,
the journey will be purposeful and you'll have more than you need.
Yours is a life that's blessed," He continued on...

"Soon enough I'll show everyone.
You must stay strong and not blame me.
Once you were blind and now you can see.
The wisdom you acquired will help you understand
all this work I have planned.
I know the lessons were hard to take.
You will complete your life's mission, make no mistake!
There's so much work that needs to be done,
now open your heart and allow the white light to come.
I believe you're ready, I chose the right one."

And just like that the lightning flashed and He was gone.
His next words the deepest, and the last words to come...
"Always remember, I love you My Son."

Rebirth of Light

As the tears of acceptance,
those of which follow the rain
of frustration stream down my face,
I discover that they are quickly absorbed
into the beautiful blue sky above me
that will form the ominous, grey clouds of misfortune,
that which shall become the darkest days in someone else's life.
I feel an overwhelming sense of sorrow
as I come to understand, only now,
the pain and loss these types of catastrophic
storms deliver upon impact.
I bear great empathy for those who have
no awareness of such pending doom.
As for now, I sit watching and waiting.
The tops of the trees billow and sway
as a gentle breeze whispers to them as it softly rolls by.
The sky continues to clear, in the distant haze,
I see an arch forming that spans across
the land and kisses the eerily lit sky.
A brilliant spectrum of color appears,
a vibrant, luminescent reminder that better days
shall chase down such mystical wonders
and once again restore my faith.
As all things unpleasant shall pass,
all of the tears that have rained down
upon my soul shall at some point inspire a greater happiness,
out from within my spirit,
a blinding ray of sunlight shall break through the clouds.
A bountiful optimism shall flourish
in such light and a wonderful life shall be reborn once again.

For the Dawn Beckons

For the dawn beckons to dare thee yet again, as I arise to once again challenge the infinite questions put before thee by the undaunted minds of far greater men…I find myself in the springtime of my life.

Is it the unbridled task of humans to create their own personal goals or is it fate that shall deliver them, should they choose to follow their spiritual souls? Is it our life's ambition to define and then attempt to comprehend the purpose of our individual mortal existences and then have to repeat those very painful lessons over and over again? Perhaps, I am over thinking all of this. Why dare to question ever so much? After all, I hold myself in contempt. Yes, my behavior is outrageous! I am condemnable by my own admission, I am guilty!

For in my faith I no longer trust. There shall be no prosperity from that which I invest, for within the deepest of my defiant emotions, the battle ensues and all my courage shall be put to the test. As for this bewildered warrior and his insurmountable quest, whose insidious existence now lies shattered as the menacing vultures pick at what little there is left.

His Book spoke only of the promise of eternal freedom. I find the gilded pages to be filled with nothing more than outrageous, mythical, mindless madness regurgitated by those who choose to use such words in defiant meaning, the so called followers and prophets, the contemporary disciples themselves, who shall bring order to the disorderly masses and spare us all from the impending mayhem. While thine own cynical laughter is expelled, echoing within the cell of thy human imprisonment. Thy rotting, oozing flesh stings beneath the rusted shackles that bind thee. Thy torn bloodied blisters once filled with societal disease stream down my limbs spreading the infection intended to impose further punishment upon those who refuse to conform and submit to such ideals.

The vultures continue to circle over- head.

Where shall thy freedom be found? That which I contrive as a mere thought within my own living hell. The birth of a mind-set, an instinctive notion, that my mortal existence has a higher spiritual purpose of which I intend to expose. Perhaps, a realm, beyond this place, somewhere deep into the undiscovered, boundless heavens. Where the darkness shall fold over and each of its corners shall gently touch to which thy endless beam of light shall speed. Immeasurable by time, infinite night shall be observed at the center of immense nothingness. The boundless eternity awaits. None of the philosophical, spiritual or scientific wisdoms shall I ever presume to completely comprehend as I process all I consume in the great depths of my mind. For the mystery of our existence shall remain as such for fear of the unimaginable truths.

I shall continue to resist the agony of my captivity. I shall create a place within thy own soul, a sanctuary of solitude where I shall quietly heal another of life's brutal wounds. Of thy own will, thou shall put forth a courageous, unrelenting effort to conquer and restore thy birth right of freedom, for thy ascent into conquest remains eminent.

And of the critics who eagerly attempt to pry freedom from thy existence, whose hypocrites serve only as destructive influences in an attempt to realign thee in the societal phoniness that they have mutilated and disembodied in the most contemptuous of ways. Their behavior inexcusable, their ignorance intolerable, such righteous existences hiding beneath the skirt of conformity, always able to justify their own hypocritical existences. I shall never allow myself to stand in the shadow of such judgment, in such a hypocorism.

My life my own!

My words shall not be censored, for I speak out upon the shore of my birth place, tis thine liberty to do so. I have accepted my over-indulgent life of entitlement as an American in some small part. I admit I engaged the hypocrisy, however, without any true loyalty, merely an attempt to survive among the ideological menaces. I obviously brought upon myself tremendous cultural responsibilities which apparently, are a component of the economic structures and values associated with such a repressed culture, never defining a significant difference between their religious fears and the political rhetoric, the boundaries of their reality. I must also express clearly, that it is not my purpose to mock God. Contrary, I honor the wondrous soul that hosts my human spirit. For I believe I have a far greater understanding of the power and purpose of such an awesome presence. It is the contorted twisted use of the meanings of such words that offend me and denounce my opinions. The hypocritical imposition and those who dare in a contemptuous way to distort the meanings of such profound words and then attempt to profess that they have solicited and established a personal relationship and a coherent understanding of such divine wisdoms in an attempt to create a digestible human image for those to behold in such fear. For they, shall never hold the hand of God and their time to honor themselves shall not be eternal.

The haunting screech of the looming vultures echo in the distance.

However, I continue to engage in a futile struggle with my own conscience, for it has become vividly obvious that I have allowed the very seasons of my life, all those beautiful years, all those wonderful moments, to mindlessly slip by, as I continued my relentless pursuit of the elusive notion of such freedom.

Should I now fear that which I alone, secretly brought upon thy self? For I, dared fate to have its laugh during those nights when I looked down upon a younger moon. Yes, I recall its fury and the destruction of its powerful effects as the tides of my life rose high above that which I believed I could sustain with my own abilities.

I can still hear the echoes of my past interned laughter as the waves crashed upon the shore of defiance, and yet again, thine freedom eluded thee, for I have not been forsaken. Perhaps, I am bitter now, however, I remain optimistic. For the moon shall show its face once again, a sigh of contentment shall be expelled from thy own breath.

The vultures shall retreat and ascend, to return to the stars.

Perhaps, just this once, I shall smile at the face of the winter moon and the dawn shall beckon to dare thee no more. For alas, thine freedom is at hand.

Peremptory Reality

I am beginning to see my life realistically.
Not as a matter of maturity or growth,
not as a well-earned level of wisdom or even confidence,
none of which have been derived from book or the journey itself.
I speak of a blue print of sorts, a divine plan, etched into every soul,
a predetermined path and outcome.
Spiritually or scientifically speaking, I am what I am.

Coming to terms, or shall I say, succumbing to the what is and what
can never be changed or rearranged, is in itself, a grim reality.
Nonetheless a truth is discovered.
Perhaps each life affects another and I'm paying a penance for the
selfishness or circumstances of a previous life.
Perhaps it's the sadistic humor of the Almighty,
who knows, none shall be the wiser consciously.
I trust that the debt has been paid with interest,
for my blood has spilled, my flesh has been torn and burned,
my spirit assaulted and shattered.

The overwhelming sadness and the length of the obvious scars are
receipt of payment and my dreams have been levied in lieu of the
uncollected taxes.
So then, after all is said and done, after all I gave, the time, the
extraordinary effort, all that I loved and my patience,
for all that I invested; I currently yield a wealth of deep despair.
Even now I feel it, but I'm beginning to let it go,
the anger and the rage slowly fade.
Yes, I'm beginning to see my life realistically.
I never really had it all under control in my life and that lesson took an
entire lifetime to learn.

Letting go of the controls is a truly difficult task for any human but there has to be a means to an end and something has to be done to stop the pain.

Accepting the truth is the first step in my current journey.

The acknowledgment of age and the erosion of time are the most obvious to see in the reflective image of oneself.

Willfully, my strength and motivation subtly diminish.

What is there to hope for and dream about?

Without this, there is no pain.

The toxicity turns into the anxiety that infects my soul
and at some point spread throughout my body and mind,
paralyzing the anticipated pleasures of life.
I conclude there shall never be a cure,
nor shall any prayers of desperation be answered.

So then perhaps it would be wise to let all that I imagined,
all that I hoped for finally escape my grasp.
I must accept my life for what it is
and grow old quietly and anonymously.
I shall surrender courageously to the peremptory reality of all my tomorrows and wait patiently for the darkness to fall upon me.
I am beginning to see my life realistically.

November Moon

I stand upon the south eastern shore
staring out to where the sky meets the horizon.
My feet are drawn down into the sand as the
powerful sea withdraws and pulls away.
Dusk signals the end of another embattled day
as the blazing red sky fades to the west.

A cool gentle breeze brushes my shoulders
as I pause to reflect upon my current state of affairs.
Of that which existed previously, the grim reality settles in.
All accounts of pain and sadness are tallied then divided by loss.
Retrospectively, the jilted total matters not
at the present point in time.

For the November moon has once again caused the
tides to force change upon the shores that once hosted them.
The turbulent ocean continues its midnight retreat without
surrender or thought of any consequences on behalf of its actions,
thus giving momentary peace to the devastated,
embattled and eroded sands of the trusting shore.

Finally allowing them time to settle and dry,
fade back to light, then softly kissed by a breeze, but its time is short.
For the shore lies in anticipation of another brutal confrontation.
Nonetheless, another innocent victim is claimed,
truth has been lost in the struggle.
That which I believed I knew and deeply understood,
that which I held in great trust.
The soul, now mortally wounded, but no, not a dying of the truth,
but a transformation, and then perhaps,
a revelation, if only in my mind.

For alas, reality takes a breath and then expels that breath
of love one last time.

Then the love stored within the heart becomes the prey
and falls victim when Spirit discovers a passion has expired.
The night eventually moves across the sky.
A first kiss shall be breathed in on one shore
as a last kiss shall be expelled on another.

Eventually the tide shall mount another attack upon
the innocent shore.
Dawn shall break and give new light to day.
A bright sun shall rise high into the rich, blue autumn sky
with the cool November moon subtly observing.
Then heroically taking control over all that lies below it
and for once, perhaps, it shall settle the ongoing
conflict between the sea and the sand.

To Surrender

The sweat permeates from heat stirred within,
caused by the flames of life's passions,
burning in the pit of thy bitter soul.
Beading upon thy flesh, a flush reflection,
cast in gray despair.
The wretched reality of this earthly imprisonment
crushes its weight down upon thy bones.
For I, am eternally entombed in this ongoing horrific existence.
Anxiety and frustration continue to build
immeasurable pressure, as the anguish of such
overwhelms my tortured imagination of what could have been.

To this, I surrender.

For the fierce forces of fate itself, plots thy miserable, inevitable
demise.
For all that ever existed, all that exists now, and all that shall ever be,
simply is as fate shall have it.
Tortured in this life and that of past lives,
one can only assume to expect the same shall be in any future life.

To this, I surrender.

Fever heightens as the sickness spreads from thy soul to thy spirit.
Beads of sweat blend into the tears that fall from these lifeless eyes,
as blurred vision distorts the ugliness of what is.
The stench of rotting flesh fills the toxic air,
the vapors of past dreams diminish the light.
Shadows of the bleak, haunted past now hide
in the pitch of all the blackened, charred remains of the hopes of a
greater tomorrow.

To this, I surrender.

A time to surrender thyself to the light has passed.
Abandoned by self, thy will, shattered into sharp shards,
I bleed now in the face of fate that lurks in the thick,
murky night's darkness.

To this, I surrender.

Take thy hand and lead thee astray, immersed in bitter hate and rage,
bathed in blood and pain, swaddled in the coarse,
abrasive cloth of great defiance.
Thy life, a gift, and one lived in vain.

Go Now

The world shall not come to you.
You must give of yourself to the world.
You must allow the gifted light within yourself
to warm the frozen souls of others.
Go now!
Fear not the ridicule, open your heart.
Fear not the pain, open your soul.
Fear not the isolation, free your spirit.
Fear not the condemnation, you are strong.
For it is your birth right to heal.
Go out among them, for they called you.
Fear not the ground beneath you,
for it is solid and your path is clear.
Go now; give of yourself to the world.
Help those who cannot help themselves.
Go now!
The world shall not come to you.

The Winds of Passion, Wisdom and Woe

For the twisting, howling winds of woe shall be sent forth upon thee.
Behold the innocent flickering ember as it quietly smolders,
peering through its tumultuous past.
Great rage explodes suddenly without fear of consequence
for its cynical, psychologically displaced actions.
Spawning an intense inferno, an extraordinary, unpredictable,
rampant onslaught of merciless, unstoppable force.
A vicious force that shall strike down
the embodied spirit of all mankind.
Obliterating any truths in the wisdoms of this life,
annihilating that which he deeply trusts or ever came to believe in.
Thou must surrender now to the raging flames,
as the winds of woe fan such fury!
Surrender, as the flames continue to grow, encircling thee.
Surrender, as the thick poisonous vapors
fill thy breath sealing thy fate.
Surrender at once thy command, step forth into the raging flame.
So be it then.
No, not thee, no not thy soul nor thy spirit,
for I am not the martyr of love, nor am I
willing to die for such a contemptible cause.
For one never expects to douse the flames of passion
with thy own blood, nor shall thee ever expect to have
to open thy own veins to do so.
Your time to make choices has past.
Step forward; accept your fate, he of ebbing courage,
for you have spent yourself frivolously and egotistically.
Surrender then, surrender to thy will at once,
bleed now, for only your blood can douse the flames.
Bleed until thy blood runneth out,

until you expel thy last mortal breath,
then you shall be without pain.
No, not thee, for I shall endure the pain.
I shall bear the scars of thy wounds
from thy burning flesh as I have done previously
from raging fire storms of thy past.
The stench of those wretched day's live on as
haunting, noxious memories.
So shall remain the scars and the scorched,
barren emptiness within thy mortal soul.
Rage then!
For I am no stranger to pain,
no love shall I sow here for the soil is blackened.
No further pain shall I reap, for nothing else here can grow.
For the great winds of woe have moved swiftly across
the singed heavens of the transient night.
So, let thee be forewarned,
for a gentle breeze, a subtle sigh of breathless
passion may be upon thee.
Listen instead, for the whispers of spirit in the
divine winds of wisdom.
For its words speaks only truths,
and the truths know no flames of anguish
that cannot be extinguished.

Where Do I Go from Here

Where do I go from here? What should I expect to happen next for myself? I embrace a new philosophy that perhaps, this time, will fulfill me and guide me along that darkened path? Has this very moment arrived as a result of all those past moments that have produced such a twisted cynical existence? Again, perhaps it is so. Nonetheless, here I stand at the summit.

The total of all that I am as a man, everything combined. To look back upon my life now would prove a bit painful considering my mind set at this point.

Where do I go from here? Stagnant, this thought, ongoing, haunts me. Perhaps, I lost my determination and even those passions that made me who I am. There has to be a smoldering ember in the cold furnace of my deepest imagination. I try desperately to relight my own raging fire, so in another attempt to accomplish such a futile goal, today I came to a place where you first inspired me to put down on paper all of my thoughts of this life. I must admit, the passion for this work not only remains but somehow continues on even in your absence. Unfortunately, the words seem somewhat less profound.

However, I did promise to continue on with this work and so I shall. It's unrealistic and somehow uninspired, and I am at a loss for words at times.

The complexity of my life and thoughts often cloud my judgment as it all bears down on me. I find it hinders my ability to open up the spirit of matters of which I'm trying to bring to light. Anyway, the faces are all the same. One of the girls at the counter asked for you, she almost started making your coffee. I felt compelled to tell her, so I explained that we don't work together any longer. I laughed to myself, as I still looked for the closest outlet before I sat down, I thought, "Where do I go from here?" If you feel me then send me your thoughts, I'll hear you. Well, I'm comfortably settled into one of the green couches…I swear you're going to walk in the door then walk right by me like I'm not here.

I never knew what subject was on your mind and I couldn't wait to see what we would cover that day. Where do I go from here? It's true everything changes and life continues on. Most memories will eventually fade and slowly be erased, but I'm here right now and it was all just a second ago. All the promises made in vain. Hey, I'm very sorry about the way things went down with Morgan. You worked so hard for her and you deserved to be there when I crossed her. It's what we were meant to do for her. Please forgive me!

So where do I go from here?

We started doing all this work because people often require help. Somehow you made me into a believer. I'm humbled and eternally grateful, all of my love to you. I guess we let it get the best of us. We trade our passions for what is "Right" and "Normal." God help me! Well that's okay, I needed to find out who I was anyway, so no regrets. I hope you never lose your passion to help those who can't help themselves. Promise me never to choose an alternate path, make that difference. Oh, the music is much lower here now and a little easier to write. It took them long enough.

The blackened horizon awaits, creeping up slowly. Another night will close in around me and this memory shall be absorbed like the sea spread across the sands of the receding tide on the shore of my life. A moment, yes, just a moment, then it's gone. Oh the rage, all the bitter rage, and so it is.

So where do I go from here?

Tonight, perhaps, the moon shall light the way and tomorrow, well, tomorrow shall just be another day.

So where do I go from here?

Only a Moment

You truly believed, in your best judgment,
that you really ever actually knew me.
You claim to have invested heavily into me.
Always implying that you were unselfish
and only had my best interest at heart.
What is your heart telling you now, I wonder?
You pretended to be mentally and emotionally stable,
enough to coexist with me,
however, your dramatic portrayal fell short of the
characters criteria.
You would have served a magic act far more effectively.
You move from trick to trick with such grace and
then mysteriously disappear behind the smoke and mirrors
never to be seen again.
Your presence in my life was only an illusion and
I must admit, I fell for the gag;
however, I discovered that you're not so mystical after all.

You never had a realistic plan for yourself,
none that I could detect.
Everything you did, you said you did for me, but all
things are not as they appear to be.
You serve only yourself.
The time and effort that you invested was for your own
future prosperity.

Well, look at you now.
Look at where you are, look what you have become.
So much for your grand plans, you threw it all away, everything!
I recall you telling me that you were a nonconformist
with broad ideals and unbridled freedoms,

such rhetoric, what foolishness!
You surrendered your free spirit and lost yourself.
You even lost my respect.
That's the one thing I didn't think you could do.
I kept that secretly reserved for some time.
In spite of all the destruction, all the pain that you caused,
I forgave you.

There was so much time for all the things you said you wanted
to accomplish, all I thought that you were working on,
but then there was the real you.
Well, you can stop pretending to be someone you will never be.
I would have to say, that is the real difference between you and I.
I prepare realistic plans, keeping my ideals in perspective.
I implement the necessary actions to carry out those plans.
I take well thought out, well calculated risks,
I spend myself tirelessly for that which I truly believe in.
I devote myself to those I love and trust completely
and unconditionally.
Even when I was on my back, with my face marred and bloodied,
my ribs kicked in, I got up and stood firm for what I believed in.
No one but God himself could break my spirit and determination
to reach my goals. I shall, live my life as I will.

Oh, yes, I have healed.
It took some time but the restoration was very thorough and
finally complete.
Perhaps, it is true; I am a much better man than I was previously.
The thing that makes me laugh the most is, unlike you,
not only can I do all the things I could do before, but now
I can also do all the things that you uncovered beneath the
calloused layers of my deeply scarred flesh.
I continue to pursue all my goals with commitment and diligence
and only because it pleases me, however, I remain defiant and

independent, yet I continue to learn more about myself
and my abilities every day.

I did everything you said you wanted me to do.
What have you done with your life?
Truthfully, you were never going anywhere.
You were incapable of helping those who couldn't help themselves,
nor shall I allow myself to believe that you ever had the ambition to
make such an unselfish contribution,
you can't even help yourself now.
I have to say, you convinced me that you were all of that but the
light of truth exposes the reality hidden in the darkness of your
unrealistic fantasies and insincerity.

I have returned to a conscious reality, and discovered a far
greater wisdom than both you and I, together,
could ever begin to comprehend.
A spirit, who has always known me better than I ever knew myself.
An angelic, altruistic, compassionate soul with great strength and
perseverance. I am filled with eternal love.

The outcome of this past moment in my life was highly predictable,
so I am told.
Talk about having a sense of humor!
I can finally look back and laugh at myself
and my morally unacceptable behavior.
I would have to say it was another wondrous lesson torn
out from the pages in the book of my life.

My contribution to you and your life
was simply wasted time it seems.
I thought I had truly made a difference in your life,

however, the contrary is vividly obvious.
Your contribution to me and my life, immeasurable!
I will always be grateful to you for our time together.
Perhaps only a moment, then that moment is gone…

A Path to Prayer

Still I walk upon thy Fathers earth,
the bearer of a deep internal willingness to achieve
a much greater understanding of this existence.
I've searched for the answers along many of life's paths,
as a result, my feet have become calloused
and my knees and palms bear the scars of my many falls.

Though questions remain,
I continue to walk forward unafraid I am running out of time.
Hoping and yearning to find peace and freedom here where I dwell.
You have bestowed upon me many wonderful gifts
and I must admit, Father, I have not used them wisely.
I'm sure they were meant to be used for a greater purpose however,
I have come to rely upon these very gifts throughout the
course of my journey for my own selfish needs
and not for the benefit of others.

So, then it has become obvious that I've lost my way.
Power and greed, opulence and grandeur,
untold wealth never seems to truly empower the souls of ideological
men.
Contrary, it becomes the shroud that covers their eyes,
blinding them from the greater truth.
For now, the ravenous rodents feed from the roots of the
meek and unassertive, the powerless masses,
who follow such strife's with fear,
those good and trusting souls who easily surrender their free will,
in hopes of the promise of a bountiful tomorrow.
They devour the spoils of humanity,
however, they will never eat the fruits you have placed upon the table
of

freedom nor shall they ever sleep in peace.

So then, have I also become blinded by these very things that I have rebelled against all of my younger life?

Did I also quest for monetary accomplishments which bear no real value at all?

Was it nothing more than egotistical requisitions during my temporary human existence?

Tell me Father, have I traded a beautiful gifted spirit
for something of a far lesser value?
I fear I have become bitter and angry towards
that which I created for myself.
It's apparent that I too bear a shroud over my eyes that alone
I cannot remove and now I walk blindly and aimlessly along my path,
for this I have only myself to blame.

Look what I've become!
And yes, I often blame you for forsaking me but it's only self- pity
I presume, I mean not what I say.
If my gifts were meant to do your work and leave something good
and noble behind, I've failed you.
For I am aware that this earth is always in a state of rebirth,
as I look back upon the path I have traveled,
it seems to have blended back into the landscape
and this world will easily have forgotten about me.
This can't be the way you wanted it to be.
Was there a greater purpose?
I always needed to know.

Well, I am lost here now; all my paths seem to cross
and it has become clear to me that I cannot return from whence I came.
So I will sit here upon the rocks, staring down at my own reflection
in the cool, clear shallow water of this brook
and I will continue to wait to hear from you.

Perhaps you still have some love reserved for me in your heart.
I ask only for another chance to have a go at it.

I pray to you Father, lift my soul high,
allow me to rise above that which blocks my view.
Remove this shroud that covers my eyes so that I may see
all the good in life again.
I know somewhere out there lies my path to freedom
and it will lead me to where I was meant to be.
Grant me this freedom, my soul; I place in your hands.
For freedom is the greatest of all powers and I know
now that it is not intended for those bitter, selfish souls and perhaps,
I've learned my life's lesson.
Forgive me Father.
Place my feet upon the path you have chosen for me.

Forgive me for wasting these wonderful gifts.
Forgive me for wasting all this time.
Have mercy on my tired soul.
Amen

Just How Much

When was the last time that I said I love you?
When was the last time I told you how much I care?
I only just realized I left you alone, cold and trembling
in the dark and you might be scared.

My God, what have I done?
After all you have done for me,
hiding behind this paper mask,
yea, as if the truth you couldn't see.

Who was I fooling, perhaps, only myself.
It was never real laughter,
it was pain that I felt.
A gambler has no choice at the table of life
but to play the hand he was dealt
and survive through the night.

The most important things I promised to remember,
are now the very things I've been trying to forget.
I thought about ending it all
and then you made me subscribe to this self-healing shit.
But without the pain the words don't flow.
It's okay, I have no regrets.

So, after all my fumbles, after all my trips,
the only real love I discovered waits for me
right there in your kiss.

To see your smile, to feel your gentle touch,
that's when I remember the measure of your love
and there always seems to be more than too much.

When was the last time that I said I love you?
When was the last time I told you how much I care?
Tell me, was there ever a time you felt safe or
did you always feel scared?

Tonight I am lying here without you.
The loneliness screams, echoing the truth,

but silence is the only sound I hear.

Dwelling within myself and all the mistakes,

I wouldn't know I was alive if
I wasn't drowning in my tears.

I stare at your picture upon my wall.
I guess the years slipped by
and they have taken their toll.

I should be humbled by your undying love
but it looked so easy for you, it always does.

I struggled to do great things with this uncertain life.
But your love was my strength and
I'm determined to return and make everything right.

So I've come to discover, after all my success,
that it all has no value, it seem so meaningless.

You made it all about me,
but now I'm here without you.
Just look at what I've put us through.

Your love, a fortune, perhaps, I've been blessed.
But a life without you, is a life with nothing,
multiplied by less.

If you can, forgive me this once,
because I still believe that there is an us.
I know it's hard, but in this rebirth of love,
I ask that you trust.

When was the last time that I said I love you?
When was the last time that I told you I care?
When was the last time I held you close
so you wouldn't be scared?

I'm right here now my love,
don't let it slip away.
Don't make me beg you,
I'm begging you to stay.

We can start this life over, I know we can.
You said we had forever and a day,
and although I may be much older,
I'm still a good man.

When was the last time I said that I love you?
When was the last time that I showed you how much I care?
When was the last time I stared into your eyes
and promised you forever?
I will always be there.

Redemption of Eternal Love
Liberation for the Unforgiven

Thy loving heart lies shattered.
Thy shattered spirit inconsolable,
paralyzed with overwhelming grief.
Thy overwhelmed soul drowns in a torrent
river of tears, spilling over the levies of my eyes.
The deluge distorts thy vision, and at once,
becomes thy clearest reality.

Until now, I could not see nor ever believe
the unfathomable truth, but then,
there you are, fully exposed, bathing in your own
hypocritical madness, the inconceivable truth,
becomes my reality.

I deeply inhale this fresh breath of reality and with
the deepest sigh of frustration, comes the expulsion
of great inner anguish.
At once, the repulsive demon is expelled and it
takes its final breath, and so it is done.
Crippling despair crawls into the boundless emptiness
then leaps from atop the highest summit of mortal
existence and dissipates into the cool thin air.
Self- reverence breathes in new light settling the futile debate,
yet not a requital nor any form of recompense.

No such victory can be celebrated that shall attempt
to mask a conscious contribution to such displaced actions.
Perhaps I should be grateful and accept this moment of
peace as a form of compensation.
Of such actions, I shall never forgive.

Not thyself for creating and exploiting such a fantasy,
and for participating in such egotistical indulgences.
Nor shall I forgive even the essence of the dark haunting
memories of you that shall forever infect my human existence
like that of an incurable disease.

However, I am resolved to lay the past to rest
and never call upon it again.
The echoing memories quietly perish.
The silence becomes a quest for sovereignty.
I am aware that the solitude shall occasionally
erupt into verbal rage, but only meaningless obscenities
of which bear no future significance.
Merely residual tremors of righteous vociferation,
words previously preached in vain.

Streaming rays of light suggest the sun shall return to the dark,
bitter sky once again.
The erosive tides of emotion begin to recede and slowly quell.
My eyes regain focus, my senses become acute.
Through the haze of deep defiance, a shadow appears.
Once again, I see you there.
I reach out my hand to you, for I am humbled by your presence.
I beg of you, forgive me!
Forgive the cynicism, that which tortures me.
Forgive all the conflict and rage inside of me, I plead.

The light intensifies that encircles you.
Your finger softly presses against my lips,
for no words need be spoken.
After all the madness, after all the pain,
my cold gray existence is warmed by your merciful embrace.
I am filled with your love.

I cannot be worthy of such forgiveness.
How can you offer such a precious gift?
Your love is incomprehensible.
A cold chill races through my body, confusion sets in.
I cannot allow myself to forgive,
I lack the ability to manage my own emotions,
nor do I bear the strength or motivation,
less the conviction to forgive.
For one to truly forgive another he must know the
deepest depths of love, the birth place of wisdom,
and then be willing to surrender that love completely,
unconditionally, unselfishly and without expectations.

This thought troubles me greatly,
for I cannot offer my forgiveness to one,
how then can I accept such forgiveness from another
whom I cherish and hold in the highest honor?
How do you accept that which you cannot give?
Perhaps there is no wisdom where there is love,
no anger where there is peace, only a past and a future.
To the one I cannot forgive,
who dwells in the past,
I bid you adieu, go in peace.
Farewell.

Suddenly a greater truth is discovered in thy Spirit.
Thy human existence is recognized and accepted as such.
For all things in this mortal life must end and end it shall.
However, I have discovered that your love is eternal,
without beginning, without end.
My Spirit kept safely inside your soul,
protected from self-destruction.
I am no longer willing to drag the anchor of my past.
Nor am I willing to waste any more precious time.
You sever the links of the chain

that tethers me to the anchorage of my haunted youth.
The broken pieces fall into the deepest fathoms of
the abyss of an empty fruitless past, never to be solicited again.
Your love rescues me and frees me from the
spiritual prison I have created for myself.
I remain in awe of your strength and perseverance, your courage and
determination to guide me through this mortal experience.

Thy loving heart rests rapturously.
Thy rapturous Spirit filled with enthusiasm and joyful euphoria.
Thy soul immersed in a euphoric tranquil
sea of your unconditional love.
Thy life's quest to discover thine freedoms
has delivered me to the wisdoms of our eternal love.

The Two Faces of Fate

My strength and determination,
effectively obliterated.
The loathsome, emotional anguish dissolves
the physical stamina to assert a deliberate effort.
No longer am I able to sustain a combative force.

The sweat boils deep within the bruised flesh,
spilling over my wearied body,
dowsing the flames of frustration.
Relentlessly, a hauntingly familiar inner voice
challenges my reluctance as I once again, struggle to
rise and stand firmly upon my feet.

Only this subconscious spiritual instinct to survive
could empower and motivate my broken will.
My vision, clouded by the erraticism of twisted,
irate thoughts.

My mind drowns in a sea of jilted bewilderment,
then swept away by a full moon tide of solemn defiance.
I try desperately to focus on my deep heavy breathing.
I am overwhelmed by my pounding, embattled heart
and the involuntary, uncontrollable trembling.
So beaten and distraught am I,
it becomes questionable who I actually am!

Just then, in that frozen moment, in that catatonic state,
fate delivers the crushing blow that unequivocally
and abruptly brings end to the match.

The crowd of ecstatic, faithful loyalists, the hypocrites themselves,

rise to their feet with thunderous applause announcing with
hysterical screams and boisterous cheers, their jubilant
satisfaction for my opponent remains undefeated.
Why do they mock me then taunt and threaten me?
I wonder sadly, to myself, as the persecution ends
and the crucifixion begins.
Why do they hide their faces?
Why do they not look upon me?
They traded their curiosities and surrendered their will
for the promise of something beyond this place.
I promised myself to live the one life I know.
To embrace the here and now, naturally and spiritually,
my thoughts matter not.
The opponent of societal conformity,
the contradiction himself,
has been slain by the self-proclaimed martyrs who secretly fear death
and are unwilling to free their minds.
The righteous who believe that they are protected by a fearsome,
threatening, invisible force that rules them.
Woe to you who worship a god in fear.
You shall never honor thy own mothers,
nor shall you ever honor yourself.
Bow your heads and look away.
You, who cower in fear,
kneel now and beg for mercy for your sins.
Beg to be forgiven for your actions.
Honor the very God that punishes you.

However, fate knows only truth.
Fate shall never triumph over free will.
Fate shall intervene only when you forego self- control.
Fate refuses to allow me to rest, it stalks me.
I have gazed upon the two faces of fate.
I am neither a coward nor a hero for having the courage to engage it.

Fate is neither friend nor foe.
I refuse to spend myself for an ambiguous cause.
I am merely myself,
as fate has delivered me.

No Time for Goodbye

I know it's very late and you're probably asleep, but Babe,
there are some things that I need to say to you right now.
I can only hope that the loving spirit inside of you can
still hear me calling out to you.

I am so sorry my love, but I don't have very much time now.
You do know this is not the way I wanted to do this,
but whoever gets what they want?
All I want is more time to love you.
No one ever plans on hurting someone they truly love.
There really is no good way to say goodbye.

I must confess, I did not have the courage to tell you
face to face, after all, from the very first time I ever saw you,
all the rest of the times I saw you
and even the last time I saw you,
you have always taken my breath away.
Just thinking of you now, renders me breathless…

Having to say this goodbye,
knowing I shall not see you again in this life,
is by far the most difficult challenge I have ever faced
and is truly an insurmountable task.

I still recall loved one's that have gone before me.
I still recall the pain of loss and the haunting memories of them.
However, I cannot ever recall feeling like this, such anguish.
So, I guess we learn new things about ourselves
right up until the end.
Now it is you that will have to say goodbye and
there is nothing I can do to take your pain away.

I promise it will be alright my love.

You know, memories are like river stones,
and your thoughts and emotions are like the cool,
clear water rushing by.
The stones will always be right there for you to see
in the river of your heart,
slowly being smoothed over a little more each day,
disturbing the flow of life less and less, until finally, it
no longer causes even the slightest ripple ever again.
The memories shall remain just as beautiful as the
pure wondrous nature that hosts them,
and it is here, in this place,
that I shall be waiting for you.

Another tomorrow is beginning to wake.
The breaking dawn reminds me that my time has come and gone.
With the deepest breath of sadness,
I conclude this journey of life.
I shall close my eyes for a last time
as the vapors of my existence are absorbed by the light.

I am thinking of only you.
I can see your beautiful smile.
My time here may have elapsed, but yours,
well, yours has only just begun.
Don't be afraid; go ahead open your eyes now.
It's time to meet the new day,
for the past is now part of your yesterdays.

All I ask of you is to remember that I love you!
I always did and always will!
If you remember the very last time we were together
I stared very deeply into your eyes.
It was then that I took from you all your memories of us

and replaced them with all the love I have for you.
Please Babe, keep it with you always!
Then I will be right there inside of you.
Carry me with you.
I'll be right here waiting for you to return it to me
when I meet you again, my love.
The memories, well, I'll keep them safe with me
so we can have them together for all eternity.

The Light of Mediocrity

If I could only locate this tunnel that everyone seems to believe
in and strongly suggests they have to go through,
perhaps, then, I too could see the light at the end of it.
However, what do I know of another man's
journey through life or his undiscovered purpose?
Each one of us is struggling to define ourselves.
Should this tunnel lead him to the light of mediocrity,
then perhaps, I would be of better judgment to explore on
my own and find a place of peace, and for myself, a truly blissful
mortal existence.
Should this place actually exist, then, I will leave a beacon that will
shine brightly so you may navigate towards it during the
tumultuous storm of your life.

However, it can also be said, one needs not search for the
diminishing light at the end of the proverbial tunnel,
for it may be extinguished prior to your arrival, plunging
you into eternal darkness.
One only need to discover the warmth of the brilliant
white light within himself prior to entering the endless
caverns of his spiritual existence enabling himself to then
discover his higher purpose.
Either way, the future is bright.

Decompression
Rapid Descent

I search for the love I need to see in your eyes.
I call out to the only soul I trust and shall ever confide.
When I am most afraid and overwhelmed with fear,
I look deep inside myself and I pray
that I will be able to find you there.
When I feel you close to me,
I'll look deeply into your eyes,
and it is only then, that I'm assured,
my love, my spirit, shall continue to survive.
All that I am, all that I shall ever be,
is that part of you that is deep inside of me.

Never stray too far, be it day or night,
in your life there shall never be darkness,
only love, laughter and light.
Your soft whisper falls upon my ear,
echoing in the caverns of my soul.
Words so sweet and so clear,
I shall forever stare into your eternal gaze.
All beginnings shall have an end,
but this life too, is only a phase.
My sight shall never cease to exist,
not in this life, not in the next.
My tears are filled with the emotion of all that is true.
My spirit is eternal and my love will forever be with you.

Down and Out

I can't shut you down
I can't shut you out
you asked me to write you a love song
well, I couldn't, but try and guess what this is about.

I tried so hard to search the depths of my soul.
The time slipped by,
it scares you to think that I've become so cold,
but I am completely aware of the things that I do.
I want you to know that no matter how rough it gets,
there isn't a moment that I'm not thinking of you.

I won't shut you down
I won't shut you out
there are plenty of things I really don't need
but you, my love, I can't live without.

So I'll try again another time
to choose the right words, the one's that rhyme.
I hope you know how I feel deep down inside.
I'll never give in, I'll never subside.
I love you I'm sure!
Never have doubt.
I'll never shut you down
I'll never shut you out.

So it Shall Be

Make it so then.
Immerse thee into the brilliant white light.
Shepherd thee once again as I walk upon thou divine path.
Send onto thee the powerful winds of wisdom.
Permit it to lift my wings and summon it to carry thee home.
For now I know my place is by your side.
I bear not the strength to dwell among them any longer.
I believe my time here is done.

Make it so then.
Call out to thee,
allow your voice to echo as I walk towards you along the lighted
path.
Permit thee, thine freedom I have so longed for.
It is my word, nothing of you shall I ever ask again.

Make it so then.
Free my spirit from these blistering restraints.
Embrace thee as I ascend into your arms.
Permit thee to be filled with your warmth and love,
for only in you do I find peace.
I place all my love and trust in you.
I'm ready for you now.

Make it so then.
And so it shall be.

A Date with Destiny

Looking back trying to recall those days,
he was just a young boy who felt out of place.
With deep sadness inside,
only pain he could feel.
Thrown out to the street,
deep down inside, he knew the deal.

Only a young buck who was eager to run,
he got involved with the mob
and they gave him a gun.
Terrible strife's he had taken on.
After a while, it was no longer fun,
but just the same he pushed on.

All the pain he chose not to describe,
but I saw the flames of anguish
when I looked into his eyes.
That poor young man was willing to die.

He was looking for a new direction
and planning an escape.
He meets a beautiful young woman
and asks her for a date.
Well, she saved his life,
she saved the day.
They fell in love
and she showed him the way.

So now it was clear,
she straightened out his life.
They fell more deeply in love,

he asked her to be his wife.

Learning a new way to make a living
was hard enough.
He moved to a new state to call their bluff.
Their most precious little daughter, born in May,
his most beloved treasure,
he kept on display.

Filled with love and doing so well,
many eyes upon him
only time would tell.
He became a successful man,
as you would know.
But there was so much about life he wanted to know.
The suffering he felt inside had all subsided.
They didn't waste another moment,
Let's live life to the "Max" they decided.
Straight to the top they would go.
A wonderful life with so much to show,
he truly loves her
and won't ever let her go.

A Letter to Grandpa

As I awoke at dawn, a Black bird cawed outside my bedroom window. There was that distinct aroma of cedar that rose above the salty ocean air. Just for a moment, I was eight years old, waking up in Moriches and there was this overwhelming feeling that you were there.

Well, I do think of you and the time we had. You know, it's funny how when you're a kid you can't ever imagine yourself as an adult, but you tried to warn me, as they say, "If I only knew then what I know now," but that's part of being young. There has to be magic and mystery, for a child, there is nothing but time.

I often wonder if you always knew your own fate. After all, you seemed to know about everything and yet you didn't say much. They said you were a hard man. Oh well, so much for the thin skinned. I saw something else. I came to know your love and trust. Oh, don't worry, I won't tell anyone that I've seen you smile. You know, today I think I know you even better than I did then.

The life we live is our own and we shape it into whatever we want it to be. As for the weaker of heart, they spend their lives blaming their misfortunes on everyone else, but not you. You moved along the various stages of your life and dealt with the here and now. You were always strong and steadfast in your beliefs, it didn't seem like anything bothered you.

I wanted you to know I watched you and I learned well from you. I am grateful you had faith in me.

After all, you saw strength where others saw weakness. You saw intellect where others saw incompetence. You gave love and patience where others felt burdened, and thank God you did because that love carried me through these years.

You know I'm much older now and I'm watching my children evolve into the roles of adults. Don't worry, I still hear you! I always think of the things that were important to you. Those basic principles shaped my life and they have even greater meaning to me today. Self- respect, dignity, your work ethic, and I never tell anyone our family business! I worked hard to make my family a good life as you did.

It is my hope that I have honored you by trying to maintain those basic principles but who knew it was going to be this difficult. Anyone can do what's easy, isn't that what you always said? I want you to also know I continue to try to surpass all your expectations of me every day. I hope you're not disappointed! The time does move very swiftly and I have gone through some of life's stages as well and I'm ready to accept my future fate.

Before long the children will emerge as the new patriarchs and matriarchs of their families and they will continue on with the very principles you set forth. I'm hopeful they will remain unified and continue to embrace one another. I do believe I have bestowed those very principles upon my children and they will carry those values along with them. I think you would be proud to know them. So thank you for the quiet yet very powerful lessons you taught me. Thank you for loving me. Thanks for believing! I wonder if my Grandchildren will think of me when I'm no longer here.

I'll try to spend as much time with them as I can! I won't forget to tell them about you. Your life was very important; it had a truly profound impact on me. I'll always cherish the moments.

I'm sorry I didn't get to say goodbye, and I am grateful we had the time we had. There is no point in goodbye when you're right here in my heart. When I become aware that my time is short I wonder if I'll have the strength to accept it like you did. When I lie down and close my eyes for the last time, I wonder if I'll have the courage you did when your time came. I'll be thinking of you then and I know you will be there. By then we'll have so much catching up to do.

Well, until that time comes, I'll keep you here in my thoughts.

Frankie

The Angel Prays for Thee

Heavenly Spirit,
Let the sword of what is to be striketh thee.
Sever that which carries the blood of life
to the heart of thy soul.
Release thy spirit at once.
Sever the restraints of bondage
and allow thee passage to the stars,
for I begin to grow impatient.
The burden of time relentlessly threatens
as dark shadows move meagerly across
the unswept floor.
I hear his laughter,
he intends to mock thee,
as he does, cursed thee, the stench of
breath, foul and intrusive.
Why do you taunt thy bitter rage?
Spirit I beg thee,
darken thy vision of the wretched past.
Repress the laughter of a troubled youth.
Permit thee thine liberties.
For to dwell upon one's rueful past
is for one to dwell within his own living hell.
To that, of which is to be, I implore thee,
allow thee to dwell instead in the heavens
without soul or memories.
Free thy spirit, striketh now.

Dear Ann

Like everything else in my life that
has come and gone,
time moves swiftly back here at home.
I rode by the park, but I had my doubts.
That old porch isn't standing
behind your stepfathers house.
I stopped there to see you,
but the new owners have torn it all out.
I guess the years have taken their toll.
I regret saying goodbye,
I regret bearing my soul.
It seems the years have not been a friend,
I keep the memories of you with me,
but I'll never come back here again.
The life I chose has left me lonely and hard.
Ann, after you left,
all I became was bitter and very deeply scarred.
Like all things in my life that seem to come and go,
I'm standing, waiting for you here
but I have very little time,
I really have to roll.
You're so far gone I guess you're no longer here.
So I'll climb back onto my old Shovel head
and ride on out of here.
Perhaps, someday I'll stop and try to see you again.
Ann, you're my one true love
and you were always my best friend.

With Endless Love

That Was Then This is Now

You know what it was that held me back.
Everyone was so disappointed that I was way off track.
I didn't worry, I didn't care too much.
I kicked over the old Panhead and let out the clutch.
There was no way for you to see me, nobody got through.
The highway was open, and it's what I wanted to do.
On that old chopper, I'd head out into the sun.
In those days I thought to myself,
"Oh, fuck everyone!"
Falling in love was the last thing I would ever do.
The asphalt roadway was my mistress,
at night I'd get drunk and whoever she was,
she was gonna get screwed.
It was the only thing I ever really wanted to do.

Well my love, that was then and this is now.
Thanks for holding on when I didn't know how.
Here's my love, I stored it for you,
and you know I can't say it unless it is true.
That was then and this is now,
I always loved you even when I didn't know how.

The middle of the road, that's too hard to take,
it's not who I am.
I tripped a few times and I had some bad breaks.
I went for it all cause that's more like me.
I never knew I hurt you,
I didn't see you bleed.
I took the words in when you'd say I love you.

Trust was an issue for me in those days,
even though you spoke in truths,
but then again, what could I do.

Well my love, that was then and this is now.
Thanks for holding on when I didn't know how.
Here's my love, I stored it for you,
and you know I can't say it unless it is true.
That was then and this is now,
I always loved you even when I didn't know how.

We got here so quickly I never knew we arrived.
Now our old pickup has ladders
and scaffolds attached to the sides.
I get up early and go to work every day,
the wild days are over but we made it okay.
We're still together after all those years,
the rebel soldier and all of your tears.
That's okay, I'd do it again
because through it all you saved our love
and we're still best friends.

Well my love, that was then and this is now.
I held on because it's what I wanted to do.
I enjoyed every minute of me loving you.
I bought back that old Panhead and I stored it for you.
You're the love of my life and I want this for you.
You're still my rebel soldier and I'll take you as you are.
So ride on my love, but don't stray too far.
Oh, and that was then and this is now.
I'll always love you and I'll always know how.

Free Flight

The bandage is removed from the wing.
The inauspicious outcome is abundantly obvious,
for the ugliness of deformity remains.
The feathers mask the scars from previous attempts
to soar to even greater, new unexplored heights.
Today, again, however, it quickly becomes apparent
that flight is not yet possible,
but optimism shall prove to be fruitful.
For flight, is imminent or then again, perhaps it is not.
Either way, the winged were meant to fly and free they shall be.
So now you place blame on that which you could not heal,
nor can you accept your own failures.
One should never take on insurmountable tasks,
for it is inevitable that you will fail in your acquired responsibility.
Your disappointment shall be so overwhelming that
you shall never be able to face yourself again.
You knew all along this mission was beyond your capability
and so, for self-preservation, out of utter selfishness and ego,
you now blame the very same one you attempted to save
for your obvious failures.
All you can do now is place blame upon the one
that was beyond your intellectual and spiritual comprehension.
Perhaps a simple matter of nescience, I would say.
Now going forward you will spend the equal amount of time tearing
down and dismantling the very one you intended to heal.
Knowing the whole time you were not competent enough
to mend him in the first place.
After all your futile efforts,
perhaps, that wing did not require healing at all.
Perhaps, you would have served yourself better
to have leapt from the perch and tested your own limits of flight.

You should have examined your own grey existence
and made the necessary diagnosis, healed and moved on with your
own life.
You cannot place the blame on others,
for the failures and character flaws that are the truths in yourself.
There is no illusion that can make this disappear and you cannot hide
behind the one whose life you made so important
so that you are not left abandoned and exposed and vulnerable.
This is a hypocritical mentality and one must take ownership
for his own actions and be willing to accept
the consequences for the same.
There can be no double standards.
I would be of the opinion that the very bird whose wing
you bandaged and nurtured, is the very same bird that
lifted you up and carried you aloft,
who flew you to sovereignty,
defended and protected you and
ultimately saved you from yourself.

Forever Alone

A time for acceptance has come and gone.
When one who peers out beyond the pane's,
upon that which has caused it all, who fears,
so nervously in the boundless darkness,
within an empty room with the curtains drawn.

When the season of love, forever deceased,
brought upon by the ice cold winds of winter's hate
and the most precious of memories,
'Neath the brightest starlight shall fade.

For, matter, it shan't, who was right or ever so wrong.
When the foremost treasured flower of life is at once no more,
and then it shall be so.
For one shall discover the fearsome darkness that
such bitterness shall bring,
to thee who suddenly find themselves alone.

A time to question has come and gone.
When, the height of tolerance,
of which one should never dare to exceed, alas, hast been.
For thine life once consumed with questions of defiance
and contempt, the words pressured by thought,
are the words one should never hold in.
To them, merely a loathsome burden, who,
shall remain now and forever, in question.
For it seems, I have lived, "Thy own life" in sin.

A time for choices has come and gone,
as the fragile young stars fade into the smoky
skies of moonlit nights.

Perfect choices, are always the choices chosen right.
Of that which I have chosen for thyself,
alas, a choice, chosen oh so wrong.
The whipping winds return with laughter to their hallowed home,
as the swollen, bruised clouds begin to clear,
the haunting moon silently stalks, as it follows thee, alone.
Truths are consumed, served with a colorful glaze
that tastes so bittersweet.

A last breathless kiss, swept away in passion
by the wicked, vicious winds.
As the timid rain fell softly from the heavens above,
as the fragile, infant stars began to weep.

Perhaps, forgoing all choices,
would be the perfect choice indeed.
Nothing further shall I sow,
nothing further shall I reap.
For the love lost to choice,
shall forever more be the loss I grieve.

A time for death has come and gone.
The words cried out into undiscovered darkness,
to which, only silence shall respond.
I call out to Angel, my words, she does not hear.
Bring end to moment, for to further time,
neither my soul nor my spirit can bear.
I possess neither the courage nor the will to resist or to carry on,
as the weight of anguish continues pressing down.

Agonizing truths, incite sadistic gestures squeezing tightly
with enormous force and unrelenting pressure.
Nothing remains now, of that which could once be tallied,
weighed or accurately measured.

Seasons shall chase down seasons as often as they dare.
The soft, lazy gaze of bright summers light, to thee,
end to innocence shall fall upon such supple, shimmering satin veils
'neath the rage filled skies of frigid, gray winter air.

The deep vast darkness offers no light to the repenting young stars
cowering in the corners of the tormenting night.
For no penance that shall ever be paid will equal
the value of so high a price.
This offer I make, for I am willing to pay with my ridiculous life.

Not another fortune shall be lost to the toss of the dice.
The big traps are set for the tiniest mice.
Dawns eye opens wide and chased away the night.
Mother comforts the meager young stars
who rest in the warmth of her light.

Eyes open, returned to sight, morning sky arrives,
preceding a brutal confrontational night.

I stretch my arms out as I tremble and yawn.
I reach my hand out to you,
ever pretending, for just as in death,
I remain here, alone.

A time for love has come and gone.
As a ravenous, inbound tide ferociously roars,
then softly kisses the innocent shore.
Intimidating fortresses of towering shell and sand,
an ominous presence, stands upon the wind swept coast,
prepared to defend the kingdom's land.
Then the fearsome sea undertakes the attack, waging a wicked war.

The great towers and walls give way at once.
Crashing down into their moats,

from the highest towers top to the gritty, gray floors.
Once again, the sea shall claim the shore
and the fortress that stood upon the sands of love,
shall be seen no more.

So the darkness has returned this love to the sea.
Here upon the coast, the light abandons thee.
Beneath the stars of a moonless night,
on the shore of a kingdom that shall never be.
Alone, alone forevermore.

The Panda Syndrome
A Societal Imposition

They covertly conspired late into that starless night.
They prepared to assault the innocent
with the first morning light.

They shall instigate the demise of
the little stuffed bear
in an attempt to silence forever,
their worst societal fears.
The embarrassment shall be averted
for no explanation need be offered
for the appeasement of their peers.

They conceal their finger prints
within their calf skin gloves.
Perhaps, they will go unnoticed,
after all, they wear the same masks
that everyone does.
The terms and conditions
they seal with their blood,
forgoing the most precious of all gifts,
their own child's love.

An eerie dawn breeze blew by swift,
howling through the barren trees
as it fades into a shadows mist.
The winds swept down
out of a darkening sky of bitter unrest.
Then the little gift of life,
takes his first morning breath.
Subtly expelled with a soft humble sigh,

as the last of the sunlight shines
into his deep soulful eyes.

Something was different,
something about the beginning of that day just didn't feel right.
It seems that his Panda bear has strayed from his sight.
So he sprints down the stairs
to the kitchen to question his mom,
but she explains she was busy and did not see where Panda had gone.

He checked all around,
he looked everywhere.
His mom was noticeably disinterested,
she really didn't seem to care.
She even appeared a bit angry
as he continued the tearful search.
She acted so nervous
as he scurried around the house
like a tiny mouse
in a great big church.

This devastated, child
so overwhelmed with worry and woe.
She abruptly turned away,
for nothing of his disappearance
does she seem to know.
However, it's difficult to hide
the face of deceit when lies
cause your body to tremble from
your head to your feet.

She changed her mask
to the one with the grin.

Then she turned around
quickly to face him once again,
another web of lies she began to spin.

Oh, I nearly forgot, Panda,
she nervously laughed.
He was so dirty, I gave him a bath.
He enjoyed every minute,
we had so much fun.
It took me over an hour and a half
and I still wasn't done.
I hung him out on the clothes line to dry
so there's no need to worry,
Panda will be just fine!
There is no reason to cry, have no fear.
When you wake from your nap
the bear will be right here.

So he ran to the window
to have a look out.
With jubilant cheers
he began to shout.
It seems Panda's not lost after all,
he's just hanging out!
"My loving mother is always right."
Such a love a child should never doubt.

A destructive storm looms
ominously in a vicious sky.
A perfect opportunity to unfold a sinister lie,
the thunder exploded just above
the old slate roof.
The lightning flashed brilliantly
inside his pitch black room.
Suddenly awake, the breathtaking

sound of thunder filled his head.
Suppressing his fears,
he considers the many questions
and logical possibilities instead.
As the powerful autumn storm
continued to rattle his bed.

Just then, out of the deepest, darkest gloom,
the loudest of all thunder arrived abruptly.
It delivered itself with a heart stopping boom!
The lightning hissed with a seething angry pitch,
It summoned him to peer out
the window into the thick murky mist.
The rains fell down hard outside his dismal room
into the darkness of self-righteous doom.
His arousing suspicions began to loom.

Panda, he quipped silently to himself!
As the ferocious rain against his
window pane continued to pelt.
He slid down the banister to avoid the stairs.
He ran to the kitchen window,
with his little heart pounding
and his nostrils flared.

He peered out the window but nothing was there.
For nothing it seems was hanging, the clothes line was bare.
Frozen in the moment,
the steep reality set in.
The moment of truth in question,
what has become of his beloved little friend?
Something inside, already he knew,
but was this possible,

could this be true?
Could those he loved and trusted
really pull off such a horrific coup?

He stood there quietly
Staring out upon the dreary rain
that would forever haunt him
throughout his life of pain.
The old turntable replayed Moon River
over and over again.
Why did they do this, should I do this to them?
Criticized and demoralized for a final time
as the tears fell from his swollen eyes.
If they could do this then nothing else
in this life should be a surprise.

His tiny tears fell upon the sill.
This beautiful four year old child's innocence
they set out to kill.
The assassination bred only contempt
and unfortunately this life lesson
repeated itself over and over again.
The storms came without warning,
he never knew when.

His search for love he dare never give up.
The poor little hazel eyed boy
without the Panda bear he truly
loved so very much.

A Message from Juliana
April 29, 2011

12:11am

Hi Daddy!

I just wanted to tell you before I go to sleep that I Love You so much!

I know I don't tell you this a lot, but I just wanted to remind you you're an amazing man and I'm extremely thankful to have a father like you. I'll be here for you through thick and thin and when life gets hard, I'll be here. I'm your daughter and that's what we're for. Be strong for me! You said you would do anything for me, stick by that.

Good night Daddy, I Love You.

12:26am

I Love You so much Julie! We'll always be here for each other, FOREVER! This you can always count on, my love.

Have a good night and I'll see you tomorrow.

I Love You!

12:33am

I Love You Too!

About the Author

Frank Simonelli, born in Brooklyn, New York in 1959, entered this world meeting with illness that threatened to challenge fate's choice. He was aware of his connection to spirit very early on. Frank heard the words that people didn't say. Absorbing as much information about this human life as he could, art, music and literature were his life's passions, an inspiration, perhaps, an escape. Like so many, life's disappointments taught valuable lessons, some of which are expressed in this poetry collection. Frank resides in Central New Jersey with his wife and three daughters.